THE WALLED CITY

SYED HAIDER ALI

BookLeaf Publishing
India | USA | UK

Presentation by *BookLeaf Publishing*

Web: www.bookleafpub.com

E-mail: info@bookleafpub.com

ISBN: 9789357612791

First edition 2023

The bloomed snow petals

He squeezed against his wrinkles,

Releasing incense.

For Syed Asad Ali, my late grandfather.

Acknowledgement

I must thank my family for their love, support, and evergreen enthusiasm towards my poetic endeavours. I would also like to extend my appreciation to Flora Situ and Alice Yang for their perusal of these poems, as well as their feedback. Last, but far from least, I express my deepest gratitude for Maggie Kilgour:

The proper playwright writes his script,
But leaves it in the actor's hands,
Guiding him on, so he's equipped
With words, but not enclosed in bands.

The actor then can use his mind
To add upon the written plot
A human soul, which they've defined,
But gleaned from what the playwright sought.

Just as the playwright will instruct
The actor, so do you, Kilgour,
Instruct your students, to construct
A knowledge base that shall endure.

With me, you've not confined my view,

But offered spaces to explore
Our discipline, its every hue,
So I may rise beyond the core

Foundation that, for me, you've laid.
This violin I hold does sing
Your name whenever it is played,
Though I have plucked its quivering string:

You are the maker, you have shown
Me how to make a movement sound
A chord. Yes, much of what I've known
Grows from you—nurtured, but unbound.

Indeed, I know when I succeed,
Its due, in part, to all the roots
On which I stand, though I may lead
My stem and regulate the shoots.

To stand upright speaks of a start
From grounding forces that remain:
Though on my separate way I'll part,
You shall inspire what I attain.

As my first professor at McGill, Maggie has helped me affirm my decision to pursue literature, while also exposing me to the delights of Renaissance poetry, which, as evident in this collection, is a central influence on my writing—not to mention her role in the development of my critical thinking around literature.

Preface

A defining attribute of *The Walled City* is the balance of different literary cultures. Though the ghazal has a dominant presence in the first half of this collection, there are even more poems that follow English forms. The allusions, the motifs, the thematic concerns—they too draw on both Pakistani and English traditions.

The ghazal is the form with which I've spent the most time, as a poet. Difficult to reconcile with English syntax, the ghazal is a predominantly Indo-Iranian couplet form (originally Arabic) that touches, often, on love—and often uses that explicit depiction of love as a metaphor for something else: spirituality, patriotism, poetry itself. Couplets in ghazals are internally unified by some overarching idea, but can also be seen as rather disconnected from other couplets. Indeed, each couplet should be able to stand by itself. My investment in this form is due mainly to its significance, for me, as a connection to my Pakistani roots. Though its flow, in English, is ever a work-in-progress, I am pleased to offer thirteen such poems to you in this collection.

Some structural features of the ghazal that I've sought to maintain include the *radeef*, a refrain at the end of each couplet (and at the end of both lines in the first couplet, the *matla*), the *qaafiyah*, a rhyme that is situated immediately before each refrain, and the *takhallus*, an invocation of the poet themselves in the final couplet (the *maqta*) to effect a shift of some kind.

I've also given such attention to this form due to its relative absence in English poetry in its proper definition (thematically *and* structurally, especially structurally). Forego the particulars, and you are left with couplets, I would contend. In this book, I offer you real ghazals, genuinely real ghazals. Real ghazals *in English* that reflect an identity defined at the border of two cultures. A hybridised context.

Up until the eponymous poem of this book, you'll deal with the English ghazal exclusively, bar the opening dedication. From that point onwards, though, there will be a new context to work with: my inspiration from Donne, Marvell, Eliot, and other greats of the English tradition will manifest itself. The Renaissance influence should be especially clear.

What this book proposes is an exploration of structure in a time where it seems out of fashion, and is seen as stifling. I would like to demonstrate the liberating qualities of structure, as well as its aesthetic value. For me, working with form is a practice in preservation and negotiation, not subjugation. My practice is to take a tradition and see what merits it has that are worth keeping alive; then, my focus turns to negotiating the problems and limitations of such a tradition with newer contexts. Thus, form and structure are, for me, means of refining a crude idea into elegance, beauty, and profundity.

CONTENTS

Asad: A Requiem	1
I. Upon that Bed	1
II. When the Jasmine Fills my Scent Again	3
III. Long May You Live	6
IV. Remembrance: An Ode	7
Ghazal I	10
Ghazal II	11
Ghazal III	12
Ghazal IV	14
Ghazal V	15
Ghazal VI	18
Ghazal VII	18
Ghazal VIII	19
Ghazal IX	20
Ghazal X	21
Ghazal XI	23
Ghazal XII	25
Ghazal XIII	27
Ghazal XIV	28
Ghazal XV	29
Ghazal XVI	30
Ghazal XVII	31
Ghazal XVIII	32
Ghazal XIX	33
Ghazal XX	34
The Walled City	34

A Triad from the Confessional   46
        I. The First Confession   46
        II. The Second Confession   46
        III. The Third Confession   47
In Converse with the October Night   48
On the Winter Sky   53
The Exile's Song   58
Seven Lyrics: On Love   60
        I. The Whisper   60
        II. The Annunciation   60
        III. Elegy: The First   61
        IV. Elegy: The Second   62
        V. Ode to a Summer Breeze   64
        VI. The Rot   65
        VII. A Valediction: Final Words   66
The Wakeful Stars   67
The Valley of Dreams   68
Vesuvius   69
The Broken Coriolanus   71
A Lament for Poetry   71

Asad: A Requiem

I. Upon that Bed

Upon that bed, that bed grown worn and hard,
From years of use, from years of you and yours,
You lie today, alive, but on the gates of God;
Alive, but silent through the day and night,
Where fitful sleep, and tubes of blood, and pills
Of every colour, function, name remain…
Upon that bed, where still you breathe, but heave,
Upon that bed, where still you speak, but strain
To say your mind, whose voice was once so free—
Upon that bed, you writhe in grief and pain,
And mutter, when you can, *arrive O Death*.
Upon that bed, you spend your days in naught,
When once, you read with mirth those tomes
That fill the wooden bookshelves on your wall—
From Ghalib to Iqbal, Khayyam to Rum—
And are ignored as strength departs from you.
You wrote some verse about the greatest men,
Within a book that lies unkempt, in dust,
Within a book that begs for you again,
While you but lie, upon that bed, that grave.
Your garden nightly blooms with jasmine pearls,
Whose fragrant musk you loved, whose musk you
    brought,
Through fragile, scented buds, upon that bed…

We bring them now, for you, but you know not,
And so those buds do wither come the morn,
Unsmelled, forgotten by your pillow-side.
Thus, on that bed, you rest and rest, despite
That, once, you would the city cross on foot,
'Neath torrid suns and humid waves of heat,
Or toil from dawn to dusk for all your kin—
Where is he now, that man so known and loved,
Where is that man, who for his sickly wife,
Transferred his every moment to her care,
To give her but a chance to live some more,
As all her reason, lucid thought, did flee
For wordless sounds, for silent tears that he
Alone could soothe or quell as she decayed.
This man, so strong, has lost his will it seems,
As wretched age does canker, slow, but grim:
What is this corpse that takes his place esteemed;
What does it do, upon his bed, I pray?

II. When the Jasmine Fills my Scent Again

You live, you lie upon that bed of yours,
And so I hold the faintest hope that daybreak will
Not fail to light the world—and come with you.
Yet, every moment brings another tear,
A challenge to this faith I keep,
And hope, a sliver, wanes a little more.
So won't you breathe upon these glowing embers,
So they may blaze more fiercely, just a little longer?

At home, you're fraught with pain, as seeking aid
From those who're meant to aid you meant your
     death.
Yet, even in this year, it seemed you'd live another—
Until it didn't.

More of the IV drip, dialysis tubes,
Those pills that do not breach your stomach's walls:
These should have helped.
You swell with foreign fluids and your heartbeat
     falters too;
Your tongue no longer moves and so starvation
     looms;
Your lungs inhale your spit, upon which you now
     suffocate.
Ah, neither sight nor sound nor speech remain with
     you,
While life so treacherously clings
To what was once your body—corpse—
In all those quivering pangs that make
Your still-continued breaths!

But won't you stay the night, this final night,
Or should you take your leave?
Why do I pray for life—your suffering needlessly?
I won't.

As once I spoke to you, upon those summer days,
I wish to speak again, of anything, of everything.
I wish to lie down by your side again, and feel

The crisp, the darkness of your air-conditioned room,
Blanketed in your presence, comfort that shall be
No more,
As jasmine incense lulls us both to sleep.
That jasmine that you loved has quit the garden,
Those bushes that you kept have dried away.
When last that perfume graced my nose, I mourned
Your wife with you. But now, I fear—I know—
That, when the jasmine fills my scent again,
I will be mourning you.

My great complaint, however, is this leave
I take of you—on paper, not beside your bed.
It's too improper, too detached.
If only I could be with you, to bid you off,
If only I was not confined across the world
When I should help you through your final days,
Grieve with the others who stand
In vigil, watching over you?
Do you resent this absence in your time of need?
This shall my penance be.
I cannot remedy this last betrayal, though you smile.
But, from this distant land, I send this last—farewell.

The midnight hour's come and settled over earth,
While day has fled in dread, in fright
(There's not a corner touched by light)
Of this our empty blackness, *nothingness*,
This ending of a sacred bond of blood, of love.
These words implode, they leave a void

That's seeped with but the coldness of your death…
Your death—*my death*—no words can fit!
Your warmth escapes, so go,
Be free of suffering, thrive in what awaits;
Nothing delays you now from heaven's gates.

III. Long May You Live

With quivers and with fluttering eyes you fell asleep,
So that this final week of half-there consciousness,
And failing organs, laboured breaths—
It ceased as came the pangs of death.

You're gone—that bed of yours is empty now,
Hosting commiserations from the world you loved.
Tomorrow, you'll be placed within a bed of dust,
And sent off to the sweet hereafter while decay
Begins to gnaw at lifeless flesh.
So let me weep upon your name, upon your death.

Yet, you—you did not die, nor shall you ever die.
You live, today, in all these tears that we so fiercely
    shed
While gazing at the corpse that was your home;
You live, today, in all these memories that have
    welled
From out the crevices of these our bleeding hearts.
You'll live, tomorrow, in the ones you knew:
You showed the paths we followed for ourselves,
You bore the knowledge that resides within us still,

You were the blood that circulates in daughters,
    sons,
The weeping children of your lineage born.

When soon this day of your departure does depart
And life returns to what was once its normal course,
We will not be without you: you will be
That soothing shadow, staving off our loneliness,
That spring of wisdom, echoing in our minds.

You did not die.
You are the beats that pump our hearts,
The vigour which allows us all to thrive,
The lamp that's guided us so long
Throughout the darkness that is life.
So rest now—rest within these hundred hearts
And let us host you till the end of time itself arrives.
So rest now—rest within these lines I write for you,
And let them lend to you another life,
Eternalised whenever they are spoken, or are read.

Your anguished fight for life is done,
And peace is all that's left,
So rest now, rest easy.
Farewell, farewell, farewell,
And long may you live.

IV. Remembrance: An Ode

[turn]

My father's father—and my father too—
Where do you stand today?
Do you, on heaven's highest floor, have view
Of our mortal souls,
Or do you stand beside us here, right now,
And bless our steps and paths?
Your home, in mourning you, does not allow
The emptiness you left
To cease. All, all is empty, nothing smiles,
For what can smile, when you,
Who raised our family name by walking miles
Beneath the torrid sun
To give us bread and rice—to lend us lives—
Do not survive with us?
Now, you are gone from us and no one thrives—
Without you, what remains?

   [counter-turn]
A year has almost passed since his parting,
So let your passions rest:
The world continues, while he is resting
Beneath some sapling trees.
If he could speak and guide your grieving soul,
Then he would order you
To stop lamenting—live without that hole
That saps your heart of life:
Do not waste your existence mourning death
Before your turn arrives;
Go, sprout, grow, and spread! Go, cherish your
    breath,

Before your youth turns bald.
From wombs we came, to tombs we trudge away;
Against our will we're sowed,
Against our will we'll wither too, some day:
To honour life, know death.

   [stand]
Yes, how can Thought, once bright, be left to mould
And waste his memory in this sorry state?
Rise and stand, stand and grieve, grieve and cleave
    cold
Sorrow, that worm, from out your house and gate,
To breathe and bloom and match your past estate.
Yet, never hush your love, cage it to green
Logic, that cannot feel—no, go, create
A statue, dress it with a golden sheen:
And make your world *remember* every time it's seen.

GHAZAL I

That long-lost sense exists, although it's stowed
    within;
The urge to be with you again does goad within.

The night was passed awake, a warmth returned to
    me;
A candle came ablaze—a light then glowed within.

Upon this rosary, I now whisper—*free*—two words:
A name in tandem forms, a name you sewed within.

The distance stopped me once, but nevermore it
    shall;
O Lethe, cleanse away the fear that flowed within.

Perhaps this second chance will mutate hope to life:
Enraptured still, your Haider writes an ode within.

GHAZAL II

The sun, from far behind the cloud, has come;
The garden's red, though long it cowed, has come.

The warmth of spring has been revived;
Lost mirth, emerging from a shroud, has come.

At last, the green of earth is visible;
This precious colour, much avowed, has come.

For ages, I had prayed for such a day;
The beauty of the seed I sowed has come.

The rain does sweetly patter into hues;
Upon my lips, a smile so proud has come.

Rejoice now Haider, fortune has been kind:
The one to whom your heart once bowed has come!

GHAZAL III

O moon-kissed, near me, you exist,
When empty grounds in view exist.

What of the world do you reflect—
Rather, you *lamp-like* do exist.

So long ago, I met your eyes
And, now, I in their hue exist.

Beside me, stay, and let's embrace:
By touch, we'll know we two exist.

If you would leave, then I'd become
Where stranded thoughts of rue exist.

Beyond my reach, but in my gaze,
The stars that I pursue exist.

You think we're marred? We'll go afar,
So that we can anew exist.

The orient globule finds the sun;
Let's like such drops of dew exist.

Your Haider's verse cannot convey
That he is free, for you exist.

GHAZAL IV

When she found joy, her care for me did fade away;
When she was through with me, she burned my
   shade away.

The summer's warmth is dressed with roses on
   display;
Despite their beauty, they must be conveyed away.

Those dulcet songs do bless our ears at break of day;
At height of noon, the songbirds too are bade away.

He basked in all his love and promised he would stay,
But for those coins of silver, Judas strayed away.

Assist me, Lord, for Satan I can't keep at bay;
Will your hellfire burn my life's brocade away?

A plague on those who shun my ruined state, I pray:
I'll turn to prisons now to hide my soul, betrayed,
   away.

Although you're gone, I breathe in wait of you today:
My peace-of-mind, please snuff my hope, mislaid,
   away.

You lived in but her mirth and so you learned dismay,

And, yet, you need her, Haider, lest you fade away.

Ghazal V

The image of my past does haunt me yet today;
Those fallen dreams I had unease beget today.

I wish to see a rose without this languished air;
I wish to feel the breeze without regret today.

The fruit of all my hopes, the gift of all my toil,
Is but a silent anguish, sadly met today.

I filled my veins with all those moments that we
    prized;
I sold my soul and you, this deed, forget today.

Though upwards it does rise, it cannot meet the sky;
Our tower, *freedom*—it collects its debt today.

With every sigh, with every glance, my memories
    teem:
These eyes, by streams of tears, have been beset
    today.

With wavering thoughts of joy did I perfuse my life;
Can I, these flickering shadows, just forget today?

I pray the days we passed find death when breathes
    this night;

They blot the setting sun with grieved regret today.

The moths had congregated near a standing torch—
But, look, they've scattered now: the skies are wet
    today!

Relieve yourself of love now Haider, walk away;
Deny the plague that keeps you so upset today.

GHAZAL VI

16

"My tears no more agree today;
They cannot bear a sea today.

The pearl that fell beyond my clasp:
So precious it would be today!

My time with you, it seems a dream;
Our tale evokes no glee today.

Those calming gestures of your hands
This savage cannot see today.

Regard this heart that you've deformed;
My blood, from it, does flee today."

The curtain hides the gory stage:
An actor's soul is free today.

GHAZAL VII

"The zephyrs gust and, to us, streak it seems;
No hopeful thought is rendered bleak it seems.

Come forth to me, and cross the shimmering
streams;
By God, tonight, my qualms are weak it seems.

Your pallid lustre ushers dreams in dreams;
The moon reflects upon your cheek it seems.

Undo those robes, undo those smothering seams;
I lose myself in what I seek it seems."

A madman trudges, chasing hidden beams;
In his delusions, she does speak it seems.

Ghazal VIII

Your phantom haunts with wailings deep tonight;
With every shriek, my heart does leap tonight.

The rose has, wanting water, shrivelled up:
Upon these cheeks, freed tears will seep tonight.

My dear, my sins have not been reconciled;
The crimson Nile does closer creep tonight.

I hear the violin of destiny:
The melancholy chord does weep tonight.

The stone upon your form is not enough:
A faithful pilgrim comes to sleep tonight.

The maelstrom's strength has drowned the Ark;
The holy shepherd's lost his sheep tonight.

The *kaabah* crumbles, idols but remain:
The centre of our world's a heap tonight.

No words can ever bring to me your moon-like skin:
No more—I won't, your memory, keep tonight.

This Haider's melted into nothingness—
Go, beckon Azrael; he shall reap tonight.

GHAZAL IX

It's morning's break. To weep, be not so keen in vain;
Reclaim your face; make not those eyes obscene in
    vain.

The clamour of the lark becomes a clarion's call:
Awake, awake! Don't yearn her moonlike sheen in
    vain.

The mosque of Aurangzeb has crumbled, all to dust;
Will we still find its awe, or search its scene in vain?

Your coral stains have been ingrained beneath my
    skin;
I pray my too too solid flesh be clean—in vain.

A hateful reign is still supreme upon my heart;
Revolts have passed within, and all have been in
    vain.

With joys, with sorrows, all the troupe conveys their
    tale;
The climax has arrived… don't quit this scene in
    vain.

This life can be redeemed, so, Haider, find yourself:
Let not the dwindling sands of time convene in vain.

Ghazal X

That smile that set my veins alight is gone:
That time, in which I learned delight, is gone.

I've heard that she has caught another hart;
I've heard my chase, that she'd requite, is gone.

The world still turns, for winter's frozen fall:
My hope that spring will melt this white is gone.

Do you expect I'll bow to you, proclaim,
'I've made my peace with you, my spite is gone'?

'Fickle'—'unworthy'—'serpentine'—what fits?
The muse of love, for whom I'd write, is gone.

Come forth, dear reason, let what's rotten burn,
Till all this home—its ghastly sight—is gone.

With every year, the city crumbles more:
Its charm, that could my soul excite, is gone.

Rebuke them, Cressid, those who dare defile
You thus. Don't say your will to fight is gone!

The ocean gains a crimson hue. Where are you now?
Your word, which held my faith upright, is gone.

What memory shall I cherish? Every one
Is marred now—every small delight is gone.

Desires hound my heart for residence:
The space it had has scabbed from blight—is gone.

I've lost myself in wandering down the road
Of sin, for now my guiding sprite is gone!

What was the Shalimar has dried to brown:
The stream of pride it would incite is gone.

By wingèd chariot, Time has knocked on Hai-
Der's door: the sun's once-hallowed light is gone.

GHAZAL XI

Your face has been a glass where lies can glare, I say:
I see it now—I saw mirages there, I say.

To her I did protest, to me she did then say,
"Enough, you maddened wretch: your name declare
    I say."

Relinquish trust from your two eyes, they cannot
    see;
Remark the world unfurled, your heart repair I say!

Her silken lips do near me—languorous scents
    subdue—
Her velvet skin—it's like a jasmine dare I say!

Collect above you tempest, come, lament with me;
Convene your rains, bring forth your howling air, I
    say!

Distressed, dismayed, and still to her I trudge along;
This blight consumes my reason—does impair, I say.

It's hankering—no, it's not devotion—no, it's wrong!
My mind forewarns, but look: her beauty's rare I say!

"To hell, to hell!" my soul, fatigued, begins to say;

The twilight breeze: it sighs a rotten air I say.

Her brow is furrowed, fearsome words escape her
    tongue;
My dearest, peace! With anger thus you err I say!

The utmost joy I wish on you, O light of mine;
You angel! God!—no other has compare I say.

The hunter, yearning blood, has recklessly behaved:
His trap was laid, but him it did ensnare I say.

Apart from you, I learn I lack a place, an aim;
When clutching you, a sense of hope does flare I say.

My rivals, foes: to all she lends a warming smile:
A froth of jealous bile, and all's despair, I say!

The hunter snared the nightingale at last, but then,
In his confusion, freed her from his lair I say.

This land you're proud to call *the home of purity*—
It's but the cause of ever-mounting wear I say.

Haider, return to earth, your follies must now cease:
She's far beyond your station, do not stare I say.

Ghazal XII

My healing liver trembles, blood does churn again;
To fill their empty throne, my heartstrings yearn
    again.

The caravans of light, to dress this home, have come;
The candle-bearers' ancient waxes burn again.

I still can't write an amoretti, Spenser, please
Instruct me in your ways—I'd like to learn again.

I've come to see the ancient walls, the old bazaars
That cling to life. (To what will I return again?)

While treading through the thick and thin that made
    my day,
I pondered every choice and every turn again.

No one remains to save me from my emptiness:
Though late, with reason, I, my choices, spurn again.

The soul has lost its fear, the spring's arrived again;
The lark, all-wise, conveys her past concern again.

The paths that winter hid have found their way
    again;
To tread upon those pathways, I do yearn again.

The dewdrops, coating all the land, contain a gleam:
Your radiance. Sweetest Eden I must earn again.

Your sweet enigma's won me, what am I to do?
The fable from the truth, I can't discern again.

As on my life's long voyage, I have found a home,
So, to my native land, I will not turn again.

While drowning in his discontent, these lines were
    penned:
A Haider locked his mind in poetry's urn again.

GHAZAL XIII

A morning field, without a drop of dew, awaits;
Another day, without a glimpse of you, awaits.

A flock of ravens rises, blacking out the sky;
Where once were lively nests, a burning yew awaits.

You sowed this garden's early seeds, then let it be:
The blooms have come and gone—for you, their hue
     awaits.

I ran from out your clasp, returning out of need;
Today, some punishment quite overdue awaits.

Policemen near my cell, the court's prepared its case;
Upon the judge's face, a smile—askew—awaits.

I'm far from guilty, dear, I'm hushed against my will—
You're not aware? A gun beyond our view awaits.

A home of kites and daws, a refuge full of snakes:
A Coriolanus trapped between the two awaits.

A spell encircles all these alleys, all these homes;
The beauty that was lost, within this view, awaits.

The rebels make their preparations for the dawn;
A sleepy Haider, for their fated coup, awaits.

GHAZAL XIV

I should not lack, though far I rove, a friend;
They call, I think, the one above a friend.

When all of Thawr was swarmed by enemies,
Muhammad saw, through spiders, doves, a friend.

"By any means, do salvage what remains
Of me"—I cannot ask this of a friend?

A moment's frenzy led my tongue to err—
So will you, for a slip, reprove a friend?

Menenius comes, the Volscian drums still beat:
It seems entreaties could not move a friend.

My value's fallen, Lord, I'm all alone:
For very little, I'll approve a friend.

O priest, these idols, all their numbers, urge
My bows—they urge me to remove a friend.

My trust's been buried past your reach. It's gone.
Uncover it and you would prove a friend.

You could not, Haider, think to lose that bond:
For fear, you named your former love a friend.

GHAZAL XV

I thought you'd banish winter's cold away,
But, now, this hope I had—I must remould away.

I brought, to you, concerns, which you dismissed;
Do you, your boundless love, withhold away?

I cannot understand… I cannot, no:
Why does your house of cards thus fold away?

I'll scream, I'll flail, but still the tomb awaits:
Whatever happens, I'll be told away.

I broke your fetters, then your henchmen chased
Me down with dogs. I'll beat your hold away.

Perhaps I'll live in Dante's sixth, but please,
Just raze your palaces of gold away.

The new-born weeps, his mother whispers chants.
She speaks—to you her child is sold away.

The masses cheer: Volumnia enters Rome
Forgetting Martius, who she told away.

Though Haider threw himself from out his walls,
He could not throw what was foretold away.

GHAZAL XVI

All reasoned thought appears perverse to me;
Your benediction's but a curse to me.

Don't spit upon my face, explain yourself:
Your words of parting were too terse to me.

At times you're here, at times you're gone for days;
Your face appears in shades diverse to me.

A crimson hue invades my mourning tears;
This bloodied lash may call the hearse to me.

The boils have formed, the skies unleash their fires;
The dark, the locusts: they traverse to me!

My Lord, I'm sick with grief, I live to sleep:
Please, free me; Hell cannot be worse to me.

The idol's silence taunts—you've won, you've won:
Those *holy* chapters do rehearse to me.

Haider, what ails you, makes you weep so oft?
'*A weak-willed muse did gift such verse to me*'.

GHAZAL XVII

30

I did not choose to climb this mound alone,
So why am I, then, to it bound alone?

A clenching overtook my chest today;
Amidst a smiling crowd, I frowned alone.

A rose was plucked, displayed for all to see,
Yet, all its petals soon were found alone.

I waded through the mists of morning-time:
Without you, in these mists, I drowned—alone.

A Haider sought out other souls, but failed;
His corpse now rots upon the ground, alone.

Ghazal XVIII

Though blackened it may be, a leaf a leaf remains,
And, knowing simply this, some slight relief remains.

When union blessed my soul, my mind on loss
    remained;
As loss consumes, my mind in disbelief remains.

This passioned grief I know, its ruin is my gain:
Because I know this grief, no other grief remains.

I pined upon your haunting glance, your raven tress;
As days to years now turn, this thought but brief
    remains.

So Haider trudges to the bed of *final* rest:
To mark that final place, your love's motif remains.

GHAZAL XIX

On Hamza.

Before the settling night, unease does come once
    more;
Upon my mattress, blanking, I feel numb once more.

Enveloped in a blanket, thinking on my day,
The spirits of my darkness start to hum once more:

'Fattening on the musty couch, you lazed, inept' —
Fairy of dreams, may I, to you, succumb once more?

I quiver, caged, as strangers strum a dissonant harp;
They pause to taunt my flaws, before they strum
    once more.

There is a wisp of light, within it clarity;
It blurs, my eyelids fall—and I wake, dumb once
    more.

GHAZAL XX

Our loud lament now chills the air;
Our ruined hope now fills the air.

What once was thought eternal, strong—
Its changing fortune stills the air.

The future comes, what once was dies:
That yesteryear: it chills the air.

We ruled the elements, but now,
If not our sighs, what wills the air?

These ghazals cannot free my thoughts;
Yet, still, this couplet fills the air.

THE WALLED CITY

"All that I left, all that I grieved,
It was endured for you, my love:
Upon this night of parting, let
These tears adorn your future joy!"
     – Faiz Ahmad Faiz

Come, walk with me and let us view
The sights and sounds and scents that sew
These narrow streets together, strong,
And let them stretch so far, so long.
I'll let you know there is no wealth;
Here, not one soul can mind its health;
And yet, not all is hopeless poor,
So walk with me beyond this door:
Forget your pictures, newsreels, books—
Come and explore these ancient nooks
Of the Walled City of Lahore,
Which I abhor, which I adore.
   Upon this street, there's nothing green,
There's not a care to keep it clean:
It's always wet and glossed with grime—
These cobblestones have seen much crime.
A thousand, varying open shops,
Where we could make a thousand stops,
Do deck the cityscape with hues
That bore the poet's ancient muse

And wrote what found the poet's hand:
The picture of this country: grand.
Yet, on both sides, there runs a stream
That hails from sewage, with the gleam
Of water, stench of human waste.
Yes, all around, the air's defaced.
　　Now plug your nose and gaze ahead:
The mango vendor cries, "be fed!"
But watch your step, in case you slip
Upon the juices that do drip—
He throws to ground the pits, the peels,
The rotten fruit for strays, as meals.
Beyond this stall lie further treats:
Some salt-baked corn, some glossy sweets.
So come and walk with me, to learn
The hidden treasures which I yearn
To excavate from out the wreck
That is this land, this bottleneck
Of life, of love, of lies, of loss—
Where five grand rivers come to cross.
　　Upon this street, a beggar begs
For crumpled bills, on missing legs;
He is not young, but wrinkled, old:
His back does, under ruin, fold.
He's not alone, as there are ten
Just like him, scurrying in this den
We call a street, but they call home,
Where, aimlessly, they roam and roam.
They branch around, into small cracks
Between the homes, to make their shacks.

There, littered on the ground, are piles
Of bottles, butts, and broken smiles.
A sign above this dismal group,
Asking for aid, does slowly droop:
The words are faded, like the face
Of she who holds them in their place.
There, on the wall, I see a wreath:
Forever lost are those beneath
Its withered leaves. They, in it, rest,
As, by their names, it is possessed.
   Wait, wait! There's offal lying there;
It's falling from the butcher's stair:
Some chicken guts, some cattle lung,
Some oxen tripe, some mutton tongue.
There's a screen behind that shop's glass
On which we'll see the convoy pass—
We'll see our former leader's seal,
Who'll give his speech to us with zeal.
Khan has entered the scene! Praise, praise,
The cricketer who changed his ways!
From prodigal to holy man,
He speaks and reads his now-old plan:
"Though I have worked to keep my vow
And I, to common interests, bow,
They've forced me out, so I must fight
Some more, as long as I have might!
They've let the foreign devils rule
What should be ours, our precious jewel.
So join me, let us smite corruption
And kill those pigs that soil our nation!

They say my plans have failed—they lie!—
They care for power, so they cry.
I'll let you know that I am *truthful*,
I'll let you know that I am *trustful*—
I have been sent to save us all
From wretched sin, to bring us all
To purity, to true Islam…
So take my side, so take my balm,
Refuse those infidels, their charms:
If you are Muslim, *take up arms*!"
He speaks these words, the people cheer;
His rivals join his side, for fear—
At least the ones who hadn't changed
Their colours when he'd won, exchanged
Their honour (if they had some) for
A whiff of power then, before.
He'll clean the streets, he'll feed the poor,
He'll fix our systems, bring us more
Than ever this nation has had?
Or, will he, in his riches clad,
Remain a puppet and extend
His hand to those magpies who bend
For further status, through his name?
He will not realise his claim.
Is this our paragon of virtuous truth,
Or but another brute, uncouth?
   Forget him now, forget such kings,
The rickshaw driver waits and sings
The songs of Nusrat, loud and proud.
Let's part the sea that is this crowd

And board the rickshaw, to the park.
The smog has left the noon sky dark:
My lungs do heave, but let's away
Before old Time adds grief today.
   I see chrysanthemums: some red,
Some white, some with four colours bled.
Behind them sway some visual gems:
Vermillion petals, green, green stems
Coated in spikes, to guard their crown
From earthy pests—to keep them down.
These roses share the space with plots
Of crimson lilies with pale spots,
With marigolds of sandstone hues,
With violet gerberas, splashed with blues.
The coils of amaranthus stand
Beside these, adding to the land
With their distinctiveness of shape,
Their velvet feel and purple drape.
Within the zinnia's head, I see
A gradient breaking into three:
Scarlet folding into orange
That then with amber does exchange
Its place. The jasmine pearls are shut:
Tonight, they'll open. If you cut
A blossom from those buds and squeeze
It on your hand, do smell the breeze—
It will be blessed by God's perfume.
Return, then, soon; behold the bloom.
To have perpetual residence
Within these gardens, bright and dense,

Would make an Eden here on earth
And stave away our fear of dearth.
Beneath, around, the lakes would glow
With faltering rays of light. They'd blow
Their cooling on the wind and let
It, in such heat waves, dry our sweat.
Our provision would be plenty:
Never hungry, naked, thirsty,
No suffering from the summer's heat,
Or winter's chill. All would be neat.
   Ahead, you'll spy a camel tower
That guards these gardens, every flower:
It marks the site where we were born,
Where papers somehow did adorn
A better name upon this earth:
"Land of the pure" (for what it's worth).
Just seven years from then, the split
Took place, the severing that would spit
Upon the face of all the hopes
Our visionaries had: like ropes
That stretch too far and turn to thread,
The families, friends—they were all shred
Up into units, far apart:
Divided, kindred still in heart.
Why, why were we so burdened, past
What we'd forbear? How did we last?
But do rejoice, this tower marks
Our modern excellence, the parks
The complement to every curve,
Those concave bits that do preserve

A trace of art in *this*, whose core
Conceals a history of gore.
Minar-e-Pakistan: a joke,
A foolish spire for foolish folk.
  The call to prayer. It's time. It blares
From out the rose-brick mosque and tears
The train that held my thoughts aloft.
He started loud, but now he's soft:
Go, find salvation, pray! Go on,
Go and pray, I'll wait here… he's gone.
I'm here. How can I breach the gate,
When I have always spurned my fate
To worship one who never hears,
To yield to one who, at me, jeers?
I'll wait, for I've been left alone
Before the mosque, where man-sheep drone
In incantations that I fail
To understand—and now they wail!
What's happened to the beauty of
This rotting faith, that we do shove
Into the halls of government,
And further our discontent?
The factions, warring, constant stress…
Is this the faith that we profess?
We've torn the pages of the tome
That's meant to guide us to a home—
A home, a heart of purest light,
The light of God, beyond most bright—
And made up ideology
To lull the masses into glee.

We pray, we fast, we claim we're best,
But what are rituals, when the rest
Of who we are is filth, is black—
When we have left ourselves in lack?
This false religion that we preach,
Restore to it its proper speech:
Forget these acts, these mere displays,
And find what's lost within these ways:
Our human love, our human soul,
That, in these lies, is far from whole.
They're done, for humans leave that cell…
Come, come, you've surely staved off hell.
Let's onwards to another site,
As evening falls and wanes our light.
  Lahore Fort, from the Mughal days
Awaits, tall columns set ablaze
With rusty hues, at sunset time.
Let's, on the dusty pathway, climb
To view the Alamgiri door:
Two wide pillars that bulge and soar
Enclose the gate, entice our eyes.
This, Aurangzeb's request, now flies
The flag of Pakistan for all
To see while entering the hall—
Stop. What are all these cracks, this black
That coats the walls? What's this attack
On antique charm? The colour's lost,
For all it, to the emperors, cost.
What is left of once-grand ceilings,
Statues, marble floors, and paintings?

What do I know about this space
That marks our history and place?
Father and mother know, not I;
Not I, nor you, nor them—but why?
Can I connect to this, this past
The elders knew and loved? It's vast,
But can we carry such a load,
The load of history here showed?
It's filled with emptiness for me.
Let's leave. There's nothing left to see—
Ah! Do you hear that song afar,
That tabla played, that strummed sitar:

"Let all the flowers blossom out,
Let spring return to us at last!
Take comfort by my side, to watch
The garden's yearly rites unfold.

This prison is forlorn, my friends,
So tell the breeze to come my way;
Upon that breeze, my knowing Lord,
Allow the mention of my love.

Sometimes, the dawn arises from
The darkest corners of your lips;
Sometimes, the dusk will fall on us
And breathe the perfume of your hair.

These ties with you do bring me pain,
Perhaps my heart is best alone:

Those who have come to serve your name
Have left, commiserators all.

All that I left, all that I grieved,
It was endured for you, my love:
Upon this night of parting, let
These tears adorn your future joy!

You summoned me and asked for proof,
That I, indeed, am truly yours;
I offered you a tattered cloth—
'My collar, ripped in frenzied thoughts'.

To Faiz, who walked a lonely road,
No path in life retained appeal;
Once forced from his beloved's street,
He marched towards the gallows, lost."

I think we've seen some hope through tears,
That hope that Faiz had known for years,
With which he did in jail survive:
The hope that still this land could thrive.
I've nothing left to say: this song—
This soil's our home; we *can* belong.
   The streetlamps blaze as darkness comes,
As crickets start their ritual hums:
Come, let's depart for home, my friend;
The long day's task has found its end.
When we, tomorrow, wake and rise,
I hope the dawn will bring pink skies

Inspired by the transient spell
We saw today, so all this hell
Would fade out to a soft, sweet fate,
Where all is well within our state.
That dawn would spread out from *her* lips:
Her kiss, perfection, would eclipse
Our griefs with light—banish our tears.
The dusk, instead of bringing fears,
Would breathe the incense of *her* locks
From city cores to city docks.
No more pollution, no decay,
We will rejoice, be freed that day.
No factions, violence, insults, lies,
Just country-people, who'd arise
As one to end the age of woe
That leaves our *Lady* sinking, low.
Go, pray this wish turns manifest:
May our *Lady* be ever blessed.

A Triad from the Confessional

I. The First Confession

Away, away, you tyrant king, today
I cannot bear your fetters anymore:
I cast them off, I turn my heart away,
And, look, at last, I exit out your door.
Without me, are you, my Lord, left so poor
That you'd unleash your hounds because I stand?
Let me, whose life is cheaper than your floor
Of marble, rugs of gold, all your vast land,
Leave you in peace. Here, I rebuke your laws
And, from this moment, in which I cleave
You from my soul, I breathe but do not grieve.
Farewell, my Lord, my soul now rings your knell.
I will not be guideless, though I leave, because
I found a better Lord in Love. Farewell.

II. The Second Confession

I cursed you, mocked you, and denied your love;
I called you 'tyrant' and I left my place,
Swearing to never look for you above,
In the sky. Now, I stand before your grace.
Here I am once more, pleading for my case,

Bowing, announcing: "I renew my heart"—
No trace of anger blemishes your face:
You grant my plea and from your court, I part.
Why help me (I, who hate your name today,
But whisper it on my rosary the next)?
Are you, by my changeable oaths, not vexed?
Though I have sinned and I will sin again,
I know you'll stay, just as you always stay:
You'll bring your light, when night-fall shrouds my
    lane.

III. The Third Confession

Rebuke me, Lord, rebuke my mortal shell,
My mortal flaws now stop up every vein;
Rebuke me, Lord, and sentence me to hell,
Where I'll, by fire, be rebuked again.
Yes, in that oven, melt me like a chain
Of ductile, waxen gold. In that dark lair,
Remake this corpse of mine and let my pain
Bring forth a better mould for me to wear.
With what's left, send me, by the rising tide
Of flames, towards your whipping storms of ice:
Freeze liquid into flesh, free me of vice.
Then, gift me with a soul, one that will know
No weakness, but face your world with some pride.
Thus, guarded by your serene eyes, I'll grow.

In Converse with the October Night

1.

From dawn to dusk, the TV hums and hums:
"The leaking oil tanker could leave eight million
    without water.
So unfortunate."
"Chinese floods displace nearly two million.
Terrible news."
"Multiple soldiers shot in Kashmir, tensions rising.
This is worrying."
"A paraplegic Black man was dragged from his car by
    police.
The poor soul."
"Shia mosque in Afghanistan devastated by an
    explosion.
Devastating indeed."
Let's turn that off. It's but the same old story, same
    old news.
Go, open all the windows, open every one,
So autumn's drafts might end our suffering here—
Yet, when'd it get this – muggy – choked?
That is a good suggestion—leaving the
Apartment might just cheer us up.
Let us go, then.

2.

Ah, cold October's come again:
The leaves are browning, scattering roads;
Finches turn mute, and geese depart
In V-formations to the south.
Streets that once overflowed with homeless souls
Begin to clear as humans scurry from the cold.
To where, you ask? I'm not quite sure.
But what a time of year has fallen, no?

3.

It's night-time and it's late;
Of course, there's no one out.
There's us, the brisk October breeze, and streetlights
    that
Disperse and bathe this sidewalk in a flickering haze
That quivers, begs for distant summer friends:
The moths and flies.
Southwards, do gaze upon our Mount Royal
Overflowing with some pale mist that grows upon
    itself;
The mountain-top caresses heaven's grey-
Black canvas (clouds and sky, indeed… you're sharp),
But where it finds this union, I can't say.
Towards the north, some spotlights have
Illuminated this same roof, where shines our guide,
Polaris—
Wait, no, there's no Polaris and no stars:
Where are the stars, the burning stars, the dazzling
    stars?

Where, oh where have the pretty stars gone,
Where, oh where could they be?

    4.
That was too loud? Apologies.
Look: count how many bags
That man is bringing to the curb—
You're right, a mountain stands upon our street as
    well.
Oh, right, tomorrow's garbage day.
He's gone now. What's that creeping to
His heap? That's a large raccoon, I'll say—
It's got a human form? It has—no, she.
She must be desperate, right…
It seems she found some… what? A cola can?
She's drinking too? Stop it. Don't stare.
To the main road, my friend. FORWARD, MARCH!

    5.
Those houses stand on smaller houses: build-
Ing after building, this
Is all there is, no room to breathe along the left,
Though on the right, our lovely park,
Its trimmed-up hedges, trees so even-spread,
Awaits for guests. Perhaps a sight for later? Good.
Do you observe that smell
Upon the air… of coffee… warmth?
It breaks the chill
That leaves me still,
Restoring flow in frozen veins and arteries.

Ah, there's the coffee shop ahead.
Shall we go in? We'll get a drink, some food?

  6.
That worker seems so old—
Why's she alone, all alone, for this shift,
Alone and wrenched from out the comfort of her
    bed?
And yet she smiles, she laughs,
She makes the most of lonesome nights.
We'll have two coffees, donuts, and—
You want a wrap? A wrap.
Yes, thank you. Thank you, yes.
Why, extra bacon in the wrap? You shouldn't have—
Thank you, bye now, good night.

  7.
This rudest wind-gust just touched me! Did you
    notice how
It whipped against the skin?
But it's no matter. Autumn life!
The park seems pleasant, hushed tonight.
Let's sit and eat beneath that tree,
Whose leaves are emptying out
Like it's a middle-aged man's once-abundant head
After both time and stress have had their way.
You see that man that's near that picnic table?
It seems he's smoking something.
Is there a skunk around?
I'm tired, my friend… tired, tired, tired…

8.

I know a man, who once would beam with joy to
    speak,
But struggles uttering even three coherent words
    today—
He cannot give a 'hello' back!
His brother's been, a while now, ridden to his bed,
Left speechless, shut up in his body, locked in
    constant pain.
The mother… I salute that lady, every day enduring
    trial
On trial on trial:
Back-breaking, mind-draining, still hopeless trials.
A decade in the past, it wasn't only drear;
All was much happier. Now it's not.
I'm tired, my friend… tired…

9.

I'm sorry Vladimir, I don't know why
He didn't come tonight.
The boy said he'll come tomorrow?
I'm sure he will.
No, no, DON'T bring rope tomorrow.
No, no, DON'T leave your friend.
I don't know why he didn't come, I'm sorry sir.
Maybe you can check tomorrow?
I don't have answers, I'm sorry sir.
See you tomorrow…
I'll join you.

10.
What? What was it you said?
Was I sleeping?
I was mumbling?
It's cold, so cold.
Let's go home, I'm tired.
Let's go home, I feel sick.

ON THE WINTER SKY

Quindi Cocito tutto s'aggelava.

1.

The blue of noon-time darkens, fades,
      Clashes against itself,
           Clutches to dozing day—
But when the stowing of the orange sun
Beneath the too too far horizon-edge
Begins, well, all that was is rendered red,
Is splattered by the dusk-fall's final act,
As if the tragic player's read his speech,
Lamented how his folly was his death,
And, bleeding, bowed to meet his woeful end,
Where princes of the night erupt from hell
To claim their prize and plunge it into hell.

2.

This play is done, the dark-blue turns to grey,
But never black. The lamps have come ablaze,
Bathing the streets with swathes of lurid light,
That seem as fairy-fires, which let us stray
From all those canvases of stars above,
Towards the concrete maze of city-life,
Where action settles for a silent rest,
Crescendoed to its climax: nothingness.
The long day's task is done and we must sleep

To pass the time that we, in life, do keep.

    3.
But I will stay awake in vigil, give
To you my witness, that you're there
Although a blanket made of smoke obscures
Your endless allness, brooch of the sublime!
Indeed, the chimney-billows rise and meet
With grey your lighter greys, O wintry sky,
Unfolding there the pulse of city life,
Infecting what was crystalline, until
The constellations misaligned their points.
Before, when I would feel this night-time air,
When it would brush against me, like a ghost,
My heart would crave to freeze the moment rare
And lie beneath your watch, you greatest host!
In Time's ensnare, we're seldom free, we wear
Her uniforms and do her work. Our ounce
Of liberty was your tranquillity.

    4.
She looked upon you, in those final moments, saw
At once your everlasting majesty, felt awe,
And lost the wicked fear that filled her days and
    nights,
That fear of losing earthly power, earthly gold—
She found in you her mirror, found her peace with
    life.
Thus, Athalie rebuked her executioner's blade,
Defied the tyrant Joad's orders, unafraid.

The fear of God that drove those zealots to her head,
Her long-damnation in the history books of man—
Nothing retained importance for the fallen Queen.

    5.
Yet, what in you remains? Besides the haze
Of gaseous waste, you're lost behind the signs
Of our modernity, those piles of brick
That rise and breach your airy gates sans care,
Much ignorant of what they've truly done:
Deny the sweet indulgence of my eyes.
The distance, where the sun had set, is lost
To rows on rows of glimmering, yellow lights
That force away the ancient nightly sights,
The stars, the moon, the inky blackness too—
All, all are lost, so where am I to turn?
The smells are putrid, sounds discomforting,
The touch is chilled by January's icy winds.
So how am I to write of you like those
Unbothered poets of Romantic days,
Who'd glimpse upon a sight serene and spew
A thousand pretty words upon a page,
As if they've stalled existence for a bit,
As if they've captured something fleeting, real.
And, sure, they did, but eras change: this age
Is not like theirs, nor can be of compare.
I pray you, be my inspiration like
The poet sovereign had Calliope,
Like Dante had his dearest Beatrice,
Like Shelley, when he was before Mont Blanc—

Or has your old ambrosia hardened out?

   6.

Amidst these deepest days of wintertime,
No snow has fallen from your house to sate
The vast expanses of my Fancy's thirst,
Where once vitality would reign supreme;
The chasms of its hunger thunder loud
And threaten to implode if this persists,
This over-staunch refusal to just yield.
You lie beyond my reach, this much I know,
But not a cloud has graced your lost visage;
The grounds before, behind, around are green,
Not white with specks of flurries, hills of snow:
There's nothing, utter nothing in this scene,
No promise you remain, albeit hid.
I thought, O winter sky, for miles you span,
Mais où—mais où sont-elles, les neiges d'antan?

THE EXILE'S SONG

*"Only at nightfall, aethereal rumours
Revive for a moment a broken Coriolanus."*
–T.S. Eliot

Repair these ancient fragments, friend,
These members of my soul so old;
The wheel has brought me to the end
Where all I've known is broken, cold.
What once was whole, a perfect frame,
Was tarnished with these blows of time;
The beauty has been drowned in grime,
The grime of falsehood and my shame.
If I am past the mender's hand,
Then let me take myself and find
A place to gently sleep, a land
Where I, with soil, may be combined.

Though I have known this place for years,
It's not my home, nor can it be
My home tomorrow. Yet, with tears
I take this leave and bear a sea.
But it's no matter. I must go;
This city's hostile to the ones
Who think apart. We've suffered stones
For speaking out against the show
Of common faith, of common lies.

Don't bow before the cleric-king,
His whips have forced our anguished cries—
Rebuke this guise, this made-up thing!

Farewell, you ever-beaming lights!
Today I've wandered far away,
Departing your familiar sights—
They do not stand along my way.
I cannot turn to you again:
My legs, now tired, cannot move;
They've stopped within this hidden grove.
So green and clean, it soothes my pain.
The vines surround and clasp my arms,
The grass depresses to consume
My form with all its unseen charms,
Replacing me with springtime's bloom.

Seven Lyrics: On Love

I. The Whisper

I think upon these years we've passed as one
And, in this thought, I find that you have grown
Further and further beyond what I have shown—
My worthless deeds can't dare to face the sun.
So dearest, how, I ask, can you not shun
This insect visage, this protruding bone,
This bland, blank soul, which I am loath to own?
How have I won—what have I ever done?
'Silence', a voice then whispers from within,
'Your love has chosen you with all your flaws,
So give her all you may—and never fall
To such despair, for that's the greatest sin.
The best of us will never seek a cause
In love, so go, love—raze your doubt-filled wall'.

II. The Annunciation

"It's as if you're with me
When no one else is there."
    – Momin Khan Momin

I leave the pathway that has guided me…
At last, the incense of *ittar* fills my nose.

We embraced, the winter draft stole all other heat:
Two were rendered one in those moments sweet.

The moon chequered your cheek with a pale light;
As dawn broke, the sun adorned your brow with
    gold.

Vien dietro a me, e lascia dir le genti:
Let us drink, for God—let the stupor come.

If from you I am taken, wait, and watch the stars;
You'll see a blood-brimmed river consume the sky.

The times forced Sohni from her outcast beau,
Yet she crossed the Chenab, that stormy night.

For sure, "I am the master of my fate,"
But you: you are the mistress of my soul.

   III. Elegy: The First

The distant church-bell gently tolls the midnight
    hour,
As I remain awake, alert, but dour:
The coldness of the wintertime again has breached
My window panes, my northeast wall; it's reached
This exposed skin of mine and now these bones do
    freeze.
So come, my love, and bring with you the ease

Of temperate summer nights, those cloudless
    summer nights
Where we, 'neath heaven, we would learn delights
That only lived between our body and our soul,
Where two, once separate—two could form a whole.
Come to me, let me gaze once more upon your face
And let me, worlds upon more worlds, then trace
With these few fingers, as you, your cheek, warm
    their tips,
And urge that warmth, like vital cargo ships,
Up a thousand channels of blood, towards my heart.
There, there, within that port, your heat will start
Its journey down my arteries, returning up my veins,
Circling its gifts along these transport chains.
So let me trace between this pimple and that mark,
These spots that kiss your skin, within this dark—
These spots that shine so bright against your
    moonlike skin,
Like stars on the black canvas as they spin.
Give me their light! Shine, shine so bright, and guide
    me right
Within this wayward sea of blind-deaf Night.
Therefore, come to me, bring with you those starry
    skies,
Those million brilliant sparks by which I rise.
Together, we shall thrive amidst the seeping cold,
And forge our fates, that wax, as one, past gold:
My dear, when you stand before me, we'll
    embrace—kiss…
We'll lock our eyes and banish this abyss.

IV. Elegy: The Second

For all who come to breathe their final breath,
The wheel of fortune halts and welcomes death;
What may await for them within that sleep,
Their final place defines—they'll laugh, or weep,
But all is said and all is done by luck:
The wheel will destine them, with it they're stuck.
If they are blessed, then heaven will be theirs;
If cursed, then hell awaits with fiery airs—
That's if indeed these words I've said prove true…
If not, then come what may, let fortune brew
Their future, guide them over that dark hill.
My wheel, my love, was almost at a still:
It sighed, and sighed, and sighed—and so I held
My breath, to stop it from being expelled.
And then you came, and there you saw my wheel
Rolling so slow, like blood that's to congeal.
You brought the heat of love, through but a kiss,
And let the viscous melt, with that same kiss,
Restoring life within that wheel—the speed
That I should not have lacked, which I did need.
Now, since at last I cherish peace with you,
I ask: come, dye me in your every hue!
Your eyes, I swear, those darksome orbs brought
    light,
Just as your tresses ushered in this night—
The raven sky, beneath which we two lie,
With hand in hand, face by face, eye to eye.

Let all the world turn static, let me stay
And welcome every morning in this way!
I swear, so long as this, my wheel, will turn,
It shall be by your leave, which I will earn;
So, I, my dear, will work to match your heart,
To treat you well, to never fall apart,
Until the world would our love discuss—
Until old Death would scorn to sever us.

   V. Ode to a Summer Breeze

Come, from your land, so far away,
Come to me: breathe against my chest
And let me breathe you in. And stay:
Two forms shall melt to one that's best.

The torch shall then the charcoal kiss,
Igniting rocks of black with cries
Of searing, sizzling, crackling bliss:
So waves of gold and blue here rise.

But—ah!—this flame must be concealed,
Within an orb that's clear for us,
But still obscure and unrevealed
So none will think to e'er discuss

This secret that we share, this light,
This passion that we know, alone,
This truth that lets us rule the night—
The night that now, as one, we own—

It blazes still, without a break,
And that is all—its absence pains.
Unseen, it forms the fiery lake
That fills the blood within our veins.

Come to me, purge away this snow
That cascades down, with rain, to freeze
The once-green trees, the rock below:
Extinguish winter, summer breeze!

    VI. The Rot

Just as a worm that leaves the earth in rain,
But fails to burrow prior to the sun,
Is left to dry and wallow in that pain
Until what's left is but a pinkish stain,

So I, a worm, now dry with every day
That passes since our union failed:
My smile has died, my mind does further fray,
For what am I, if you have gone away?

My foolish heart at once expects your love,
But fears as well that it has lost it all;
O foolish heart of mine, stop: do not shove
My ribs, you mustn't ask my blood to move.

When I have built my house around your law,
When I would rise to see you, not the sun—

Then what remains, since thoughts of you withdraw
Me from the world, to ice that shall not thaw?

VII. A Valediction: Final Words

Though we have passed the fork that splits the road,
To send us off to separate futures, know
My heart has peace, that I could sing an ode
To all those times that did between us flow.
Against my will, I had to let you go,
Like Troilus had poor Cressid, for what's good:
But now you've found yourself, and still you grow—
So thrive! Forget that, by you, I once stood.
The inkpot's dry, replacements out of sight,
So let me send these final words your way:
O dearest love, I wanted every day
That we could have, though very few were penned.
Perhaps another life, we'll have the ink to write
This chapter that, today, has reached its end.

THE WAKEFUL STARS

The night will pass in but distress,
As silent hums of death do creep:
Your pallid gleams excite my eyes,
So stars, forget me—sleep!

Until the break of dawn brings warmth,
My wait will helpless, hopeless stay;
Alas, this is my fortune sad,
So stars, forget me—sleep!

Another day has slipped my hand,
No one has pitied, graced this home:
My strength departs, and you shall too,
So stars, forget me—sleep!

Against this dark, you show my face,
So wretched, sullied from these years;
You've lit the path, it's empty still,
So stars, forget me—sleep!

I promise, I will sleep tonight,
These restless times will soon be gone;
And yet, your rays do plead me back,
So stars, forget me—sleep!

THE VALLEY OF DREAMS

I do desire, beneath the moon,
Your loving cradle and caress.
So please arrive, so please come soon:
Relieve me of the world's distress.

Consume me here, I beg of you,
And take me where my peace awaits.
I will forget the breaths I rue,
Just as I'm taken past your gates.

I'll meet some angels who will sing
And cleanse the worldly from my mind.
The emptiness I'll face will bring
A joy that I could not yet find.

I shall be free then: when you come,
The shackles binding me will break.
So blind my sight, and freely strum
My heart—relieve me of my aches.

Upon this night, come softly, sleep,
I now surrender both my eyes.
Beyond this dark, I ask you: keep
This soul, to suffocate its cries.

VESUVIUS

The dirge was singing for the dead,
As markets hummed with winter life;
The sayer warned that doom did loom,
But potters laughed and sold their urns.
The good, the bad, the fine, the cruel,
It all perfused the Roman square—
The Roman square that had its light.

The tremors strike, the vases fall,
The lead-laced vases, glossed with red;
Their history, their art—it hits
The quaking earth and shatters out,
Transforming into painted shards:
These Roman marks are sent to earth,
As the Roman square loses light.

The holy ash, it spreads again,
It spreads towards the city now…
The smoke, the smoke, it fills the air,
And blocks the sunbeams from this town:
So off the rolling tufts of grey,
The Roman square is led to night—
The Roman square is drained of light.

The beggar flees, but falls to rain,
A heavy rain that buries him;

The merchant hoards his little gems,
And freezes as the pumice lands:
Some left and lived some more… some stayed,
Entombed, enshrined, eternally,
In the Roman square's deathly light.

THE BROKEN CORIOLANUS

Volumnia kneels, Virgilia kneels,
Young Martius kneels—they weep.
So Martius, anguished, also kneels:
The skies at this do weep.

"O mother, mother, how may I
Go into Rome? I yield!
You've won, my mother, but… but I
Have lost. My life I'll yield!"

Volumnia hears him, turns around,
And enters Rome with cheer;
While Coriolanus turns around
To men who cannot cheer.

Defeated by his former home,
Coriolanus turns back;
As he's unwelcome in his home,
To Antium he heads back.

By jealous hands he's stabbed, he dies—
On cold-seeped floors he lands.
This broken Coriolanus dies,
Alone, in foreign lands.

A LAMENT FOR POETRY

"…choose for thy command
Some peaceful province in acrostic land.
There thou may'st wings display and altars raise,
And torture one poor word ten thousand ways."
    – John Dryden

1.

Forget the 'verse' that runs without its feet;
Forget the poems that you see today:
To write (that is, to teach and to be sweet)
Is not a simple task, not children's play,
But, rather, proper craft that lends a way
To find some beauty in a fairy plain
While all the world just trudges to decay.
That beauty holds existence—joy and pain—
But, take the beauty out, and nothing's left to gain.

2.

Give me music with food—away with prose
That masquerades where poetry resides.
Express in words your life, your love, your woes—
And heed the waves of rhythm, all its tides:
So yield yourself to iambs, trochees—sound guides
The feeling of your words and lets me hear
Prophetic lies much better than divides
In lines (bereft of sense, but still held dear).

I loath sweet words alone; I love to please my ear.

   3.

Perhaps, you think, "from rhyme I lose my will,
I find myself in shackles, feeling drowned."
Of course, those thoughts that, from your mind, will
    spill
Onto a page cannot depend on sound—
Which soon will seem to readers mouldy, browned.
No rhyme or metre aids the empty line.
Yet, think: when lines have worth, they should be
    crowned
With sonic laurels that will be their sign
That they are poems, not some gilded prose design.

   4.

Now, let us think together: if I leave
My stanza and randomly break my lines here,
Here,
And here,
To make a meaning out of petty change—

   5.

Or, better yet,
start each line with lowercase letters… no,
use lowercase letters exclusively, to show how
    strongly
i am rejecting traditions,
and say 'i carry your heart with me':
am i writing a poem with skill?

or is this simply a glorified title to give to prose
that lacks a sense of identity
(just
as
we
all
should
because
we're
modern
or
post-
modern
people)?

6.
if i think that my shower time musings
are so great
that they should be vomited
into times new roman on a document,
for my *milk and honey,*
then am i a
poet
just because i make poetry
accessible?

7.
if i write prose without any punctuation and put
some pretty images here and there explaining how 'i
smell tulips and narcissus' in the air or how

everything is 'on fire' then am i writing poetry or
rather laudable prose that is exceptional in all but its
classification

   8.
No, no, no! This cannot be called a verse.
When gold is given freely, sweet delight
Is made unsweet, and sent off in a hearse;
And so it is with poems, which we smite
Through upstart poets, minds that lack the might
And skill to carry forth this ancient art
Practised by greats, like Spenser—stars more bright
Than all these modern worms that bleed their heart
With unmusical whims, playing the poet's part.

   9.
For us who cringe at this, there's no relief.
We all should know as sound defines a song,
It makes a poem. We must not give such grief
To Donne, Marvell, or Milton, yet we long
To make their craft so free—to let a throng
Of hopeless writers take the stage and steal
The grandeur of the rare with but their strong
Egos, discordant lines, which hold appeal
For those who have forgot what's good (it makes
    them reel).

   10.
To write with form: it does not ruin access;
Instead, it makes a reader think and grow.

When few can sit and read without some stress,
When few can find themselves a focused flow,
Think how a witty rhyme, a metre's woe,
Can feed the mind with thoughts beyond what's
    seen,
Or raise an image from a distant shadow
To an enthralling shape that makes us keen
Participants, immersed as such within a scene.

   11.
Yet, not all blame, I yield, is on the horde
Of third-rate poets: ah, the tastes of time
Have left Calliope forgotten, stored
Away in attics full of books and grime.
The poet, be they great or be they slime,
Has no attention or respect—is squeezed
To dusty circles. Those who cannot rhyme,
In this crisis, with no one to displease,
Have built their dusty thrones, have brought their
    pests, disease.

   12.
And even worse, I find, to but impress
We've sold our souls—our verse—to money, greed:
"If we do wish to ever find success
Within this modern world, then, yes, indeed,
There is a cost." Well, many have agreed,
And so do I, that for our bread and tea,
There is this cost. But why obey the lead
Of charlatans who lack creative glee

And market all their lines like leaves upon a tree?

   13.
To let the garbage rise beyond its place
Is not a crime—but as it, in its rising,
Conceals the diamonds, sapphires (all their trace)
Deep underneath itself, our too-poor prizing
Of it should cease. We should be re-devising
What forms and structures make our precious
    stones,
To block what's cheap. In song (it's unsurprising),
The fame of overused, synthetic tones
Has left all talent, effort, languishing to bones.

   14.
Now, I will say—my stance, I hope, made clear—
That not all lines, sans metre, are a waste:
Many are great: take those that do appear
In Eliot's verse, or Yeats'—figures with taste
Enough (and tact) to form well-thought, well-paced,
Unusual lines—suffused with sounds that tell
The world that they are verse, not prose. Defaced
Are all such peerless works by frauds that sell
Their average prose as *free verse*, ringing poetry's
    knell.

   15.
This is my sorrow, dressed in honest rage,
Regarding those poets that tear the thread
Defining poetry, that make this age

The darkest one this choking art has tread—
No sturdy garb, no cap to hide its head
From thunder, rainstorms, hailstones… and no clear
Guardian to shield its naked form from red.
So heed my words, revive our state from drear;
The death of poetry is creeping close, I fear.